Mike and Hilary Wreford's

OKEHAMPTON
COLLECTION III

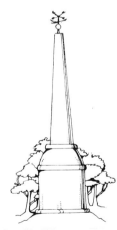

OBELISK PUBLICATIONS

First Published in 1995 by Obelisk Publications
2 Church Hill, Pinhoe, Exeter, Devon
Designed by Sally Barber
Typeset by Sally Barber
Printed in Great Britain by
Maslands Ltd, Tiverton, Devon

ISBN: 1 899073 12 4

In this 1910 picture the London Hotel is certainly looking to the future! Webber and Sons are advertising as a "Posting House" but at the same time the sign over the main door indicates over 2,500 square feet of garage space is available. In the foreground is their magnificent four-in-hand with Ernest Webber holding the reins. He was a familiar figure around the area as well as behind the bar. Ernest was an accomplished horseman and as Marshall lead the carnival for many years. His father, known affectionately as "Grandad" Webber, is standing below his son at the front of the coach.

3

It is not generally known that St James Church was at one time semi-detached! This 1875 photo shows the adjoining shop and house; although the sign is difficult to read, it was the prominent business of S. Drew, who traded as a watch and clock maker and Jeweller. The shop later became "Rowe The Butchers" before being demolished. Okehampton had a propensity of public houses in those days with the New Inn on the right and the Bridge Inn (now Bridge House) in the background. Otherwise St James Church is relatively unchanged, and still keeps a fatherly watch on the town.

West Bridge in 1850 was much different than it is now, and certainly would never be suitable for today's motor transport, despite the bypass! West Bridge over the centuries has been known as Bear, Beare or Beere Bridge and was so named because the funeral procession had to make its mournful way across onto the hillside Church. The bridge had been built in 1831 as a date in the weather-beaten granite indicated. It was in those days only for pedestrians, livestock and horse-drawn vehicles, but it would probably, with

its sturdy construction, have lasted for ever. However, the increasing traffic made it necessary for it to be demolished and finally, after being delayed by the war, this came to fruition and the bridge as we see it today was erected in 1956. The bridge had lasted 125 years. Incidentally, in the seventeenth century it was recorded that 'six hundred yards of causeway was paved leading to the church and from Bear bridge and amounted to £11.13s.10½d'

This was no doubt a colourful scene as Okehampton celebrated Queen Victoria's Jubilee in 1887 in lively fashion. It is looking east and the bank building and the Plume of Feathers are somewhat different than today. This was well before the Arcade was constructed and is one of the few photographs looking east along Fore Street, which does not feature St James Church! Ten years later a second festival, known as the Diamond Jubilee, celebrated the longest reign of any British Monarch, and a further demonstration of Okehampton's loyalty to the Crown.

MEMORIAL SERVICES.

OKEHAMPTON.

His Worship the Mayor (Alderman Henry Geen) on Sunday morning attended in State a service held at the Parish Church in memory of our late beloved Queen. The weather was most unpropitious, rain falling in torrents, but despite the fact his Worship was strongly supported by those who joined in the procession, which left the Town Hall at 10.15 a.m., and marched by way of Church-hill to the Church. After the Mayor walked the Aldermen and Town Councillors, the Borough officials, members of the Charity Trustees and School Board and their officials, the local Company of the Volunteers (under the command of Lieut. B. B. Newcombe), the Fire Brigade (under Capt. S. Newcombe), Mr. T. P. Hamlyn (Postmaster), the Postal Staff, with the postmen and telegraph boys in their uniforms, and others, whilst three bluejackets added to the representative character of the procession. The Church was crowded, many temporary seats having to be placed in some parts of the Church. The service, which was very impressive, was conducted by the Vicar (Rev. A. L. Giles), and the Curate (Rev. A. Millett), the former reading the two lessons and preaching the sermon, whilst the Rev. Millett did the intoning, &c. Special Psalms, 23rd and 61st, were sung, and the hymns chosen were 193, 499, and 428. The Vicar preached an eloquent and touching sermon from the words, "For David, after he had served his own generation by the will of God, fell on sleep" (Acts 13, v. 36). At the conclusion of the service, the organist (Mr. S. Janes) gave a fine rendition of the "Dead March" in Saul, the whole congregation remaining standing. The procession was now re-formed and marched back to the Town Hall, where the Volunteers, &c., were drawn up in line whilst the "Dead March" was played by the Volunteer Band — The Mayor thanked all those who, in spite of the rough state of the weather, had followed him to Church that morning on so great and solemn an occasion. He hoped next Saturday, when he proposed attending another service at the Parish Church during the time of the Royal funeral, they would all attend with him again in so large numbers, and that the weather would be much more favourable.— The proceedings then terminated.

Torrential rain fell during the morning of that January day in 1901 as the parade assembled in Fore Street for the Memorial Service following the death of Queen Victoria. Excerpts from a press cutting of the time, give an impression of the feeling of the passing of this beloved Monarch.

This pre-1914 photograph shows a street frontage that has long since ceased to exist.

The "Friends Eating House" in West Street was very popular for locals and holiday makers alike, and on market days the farmers would pack into the small rooms (for a 3-course meal at one shilling (5p) who could grumble?). This tranquil scene was soon disturbed by the outbreak of the 1914-18 war and the Friend Family was the first in Okehampton to suffer the tragic loss of a loved one. Son, Albert John (Jack) had enlisted as a "Shoeing Smith" and was serving with the 9th Lancers in France. The 9th Lancers took part in probably the last "Lance versus Lance" battle and the following is an extract from the Delhi Spearson: "It is very seldom that cavalry have the opportunity of engaging in Hand-to-Hand combat in modern warfare, but the story is unique, not only as an Example of Regimental history, but as an example of skill and cavalry dash." It was an outstanding episode during the BEF Retreat from Mons (the Battle of the Marne) when the 9th Lancers and German 1st Guard Dragoons came into conflict. In this heated exchange, sadly, Jack Friend and two others were killed in action. He was buried by the Regiment in a little churchyard at Fretory, but even then he could not rest, as it was discovered by the Mayor that he was not buried deep enough for French Law; subsequently he was re-interred in a quiet corner of the same churchyard.

In Okehampton this scene remained unchanged for many years with the narrow street serving as a main road to Cornwall and the west. The increased use of the motor car was causing bottlenecks and the demolition of the middle row of shops and houses became inevitable. This considerable work took place in the late 1930s and a piece of Okehampton history disappeared for ever.

Whilst the Friend Family had experienced such a sad time with the death of Jack, his Great friend William 'Bill' Hain had survived the conflict and is pictured opposite, third from left in the second row. He had been promoted to Sergeant, and awarded the Military Medal for outstanding bravery during the war and is proudly displaying this medal and the inevitable cigarette!

It is no wonder that there were smiling faces as civilians and returning soldiers alike celebrated the armistice of 1918.

The man in the foreground in Civvies and large cap is Mr Walter Bassett. Whilst behind Bill Hain with trilby is Okehampton character George Gunn.

9

This 1920 view looking down East Street shows the premises of Ruby Sampson & Co Motor, Electrical, Wireless and Agricultural Engineers. Their Motor car garage at No's 32 & 34 East Street were well known and well respected throughout the area. Their petrol pump was situated close to the road and one can imagine the chaos this would cause traffic today! These premises later became J. T. Ruby & Son, subsequently to come under the hammer, likewise the lovely methodist Church. The area was rebuilt by Ian MacCullock, and renamed Yes Tor Filling Station. This has now been developed as a residential area with the construction of The Chantry and further down Lillicrap Court. Notice the unmade road and the Gas Lighting on the corner. Allens corner shop provided a service to countless people over the years.

For almost 70 years the "small shop with a big choice" and with a late sixteenth century background was run by the respected Bassett Family in St James Street.

Taken in 1922, this picture shows Mr Walter Bassett (back) with (left to right), Fernley Rogers (Lather Boy), Bill Bassett (son), Ernest Bassett (son) and daughter Joan.

The story began in 1911 when Walter set up a hairdressing salon in North Street, subsequently moving to St James Street in 1914. It was after being invalided out of the army in 1917 that Walter started to sell papers as well and the business soon became one of the busiest and most popular in the town.

Walter had an enviable reputation as a 'Tipster' and on big race days the little shop was a focal point as eager punters followed the fortunes of their favourites, using the excuse of a much needed haircut or shave to their wives!

It was a sad day for Okehampton when sons Ernest and Roy, to whom the business had passed, decided to call it a day and 70 years of "Bassett Family" service to the community came to an end.

The Star Supply Stores was a happy shop for both customers and staff alike, and was situated in Fore Street at the top of the Red Lion Yard. This photograph, taken on 16th Nov 1932, was to record their entry in a window dressing and lighting competition and featured the entire staff. (Left to Right) Lou "Tich" Lobb (Roundsman), Seth Bulley, May Ederly, Cecil Mortimore, Joyce Gratton, John Yolland (Manager), Fred Brooks, "Pethys" Pethbridge, Richard Walters, "Errand Boy" Carter.

The shorter white overalls was obviously the style at the time to distinguish the managers. Richard Walters later became manager of the Wellington Branch shop. A large country round was operated with Cecil Mortimore taking the orders, which, after being made up in the 'order room' at the rear of the premises, were duly delivered by that well-known local character "Tich" Lobb. The price of butter at one shilling (5p) a pound gives an indication of prices at the time.

There was obviously no need for a bypass in 1906 as this peaceful picture indicates. It was taken at the turn of New Road leading out of Okehampton. Clues for the modern day Ocketonians are the houses on the left, which are broadly much the same, and the offices of Days Garage with its stone and granite frontage. Note, apart from the spread of unworried people across the road, the little vehicle on the left. This was a baker's cart, used by the baker of the day for his deliveries. The ponyless cart is parked outside what at the time was Gale's Blacksmith's Forge. Perhaps the pony was inside being shod?

It was a red letter day for Okehampton Wesleyan Methodists at their stone-laying ceremony on 27th May 1903. This picture shows the laying of the corner stone by Mr William Beer – altogether 52 foundation stones were laid. The day started with an early morning prayer meeting in the West Street Chapel followed by an 11:30 a.m. service. The luncheon for 200 guests was held in the Market Hall with the Mayor, Dignitaries from all over Devon and John Spear our MP. It continued with an evening meeting where it was revealed that £1,000 had been raised during the day, a considerable sum for 1903. It is interesting to note that in addition to the church for a congregation of 375 people, the four classrooms planned were for 250 scholars! This picture also illustrates the lack of houses at the bottom of Station Road and that the Masonic Lodge had only a single-storey frontage.

There has always been some feeling that the Castle Lodge should never have been demolished, and the above photograph illustrates this sturdy stone-built dwelling. In the early part of the century Emma and John Hawkins were custodians of the castle and it is two of their children, Betty and Dick, who are pictured in the gateway. Sadly tragedy was to strike this family twice, firstly their 2-year-old daughter Phyllis Agnes drowned in the stream behind the castle on 15th September 1914. Mum, Emma never recovered from this and just four years later, the still grieving Emma died in an influenza epidemic that was prevalent in Okehampton at that time. In later years John and Lilian Glover were popular custodians but alas, like all good things, it came to an end.

There had been talk and plans for a purpose-built Hospital in Okehampton ever since the last century but it was not until 27th May 1925 that the foundation stone was laid, and the Okehampton and District War Memorial Hospital subsequently opened. Improvements soon followed and here we can see Viscountess Broome opening the new Children's Ward in 1930. The ward had been provided mainly through the generosity of Mr and Mrs Joseph Rippon. On the right of this picture is Dr E. H. Young (President of the Hospital) and the Matron (Sister Clifford). Major Pat à Beckett, who contributed much in memory of his wife, is pictured on the left.

OKEHAMPTON
WAR MEMORIAL HOSPITAL.

OPENING OF A NEW
CHILDREN'S WARD.

OKEHAMPTON is a typical moorland town, with its grey stone houses nestling around the slopes of the great grey tors of Dartmoor: not by any means an isolated town, though, for, especially during the summer months, it is full of movement and gaiety, much as it was recently for the opening of the new children's ward of the Okehampton and District War Memorial Cottage Hospital.

The hospital, though small, is an institution very dear to the hearts of the "moormen" and their families, and they have been quick to help its needs. The land it stands on was donated by Mr. and Mrs. G. K. Blatchford, the hospital itself being erected (as a brass tablet in the hall testifies) as a memorial to the men of Okehampton and the neighbouring villages who fell in the war during 1914 to 1918. The new children's ward has been given to the hospital by Mr. and Mrs. Joseph Rippon, while the second-storey rooms, comprising nurses' quarters and private wards, were built from funds collected by a fête and other means last summer. Major Pat à Beckett gave the furniture of these rooms and of the children's ward in memory of his late wife, Lady Nora à Beckett, and it was his sister-in-law, Viscountess Broome, who declared the new ward open last Tuesday, mentioning in her speech that both she and her late sister had both nursed during the War.

A Public Tea.

The proceedings were simple, and marked by a friendly, homely feeling which made one realise how interested in its own hospital was the large crowd present. After the singing of a hymn and the presentation of a bouquet of roses and carnations to Viscountess Broome, came the address of the president of the hospital committee,

Dr. Young. Viscountess Broome then declared the new ward open, dedicatory prayers by the Rev. R. H. Welchman and a final hymn following. The Mayor of Okehampton, Mr. W. B. Chammings, proposed a vote of thanks to Viscountess Broome, and after some further speeches and the singing of the National Anthem a public tea at the council school-rooms took place.

Miss D. Clifford is the matron of the Okehampton and District War Memorial Cottage Hospital. Formerly acting matron of Lyme Regis Cottage Hospital, she was trained at Birmingham General Hospital, and has also received fever and midwifery training. The little hospital under her charge at Okehampton has two main wards, the men's ward and the woman's ward, with five beds in each. The new children's ward contains seven cots of the most up-to-date type, with movable back-rests, pulleys, apparatus for the obtaining of different positions, and other modern advantages; a finely equipped operating theatre and anaesthetising room; three charmingly furnished private wards; and an out-patients' and casualty department, the latter having, as in most districts where the roads have not been primarily designed for motor traffic, its share of motor accidents, while quarry accidents are also an occupational risk of the neighbourhood.

Lovely Moorland View.

The staff under Miss Clifford consists of a sister, two staff nurses and two probationers, the medical and surgical staffs being honorary. Exeter surgeons also perform a number of operations at the hospital. The nurses' sitting-room is a beautiful and comfortable room, with, of course, a lovely moorland view, a feature, too, of Miss Clifford's own sitting-room, as well as of most of the other parts of the hospital. The wards have French windows opening on to covered, tiled verandahs, where the invigorating moorland air does its good work among convalescent patients. The entire building, in its own small way, is as efficient as modern hospital architecture can make it.

M. P.

Reproduced by kind permission of Nursing Times. This article first appeared in the Nursing Mirror on November 8th, 1930.

A celebratory photograph for the Home Guard who had just won the Section Cup for the best Platoon. This squad used to meet once a week at the Drill Hall, which was the Headquarters for this "Fighting Force." They had of course been formed as the L. D. V. (Local Defence Volunteers) and initially armed with very primitive weapons, although as this photograph shows they were now well equipped. It says much for the various squads of Home Guards in and around Okehampton that the residents were able to sleep easily in their beds. In fact by the summer of 1943 there were 1.75 million home guards in the country with an average age of 30!
Back row (L to R) Walter Newcombe (Relieving Officer), Reg Maddaford (Baker), Ern Trick (Driver), Claude Cockwill (Mason), William Willoughby (Baker's Roundsman), John James (Baker), Bill Rowland (Baker), William Jackson (Draper), Victor Sanders (Stores Manager). Sitting: Jimmy Crocker (Carpenter), George Gunn (Co-director), (?), Reg Maddaford (Bus conductor), Tommy Bevan (Plumber).

The photograph includes all personnel employed in the transport department of the Devon War Agriculture Committee (DWAC) throughout the area and mainly based at Okehampton.

The DWAC was situated at the Barton Garage at Stockley with the adjoining bungalow as offices.

The Transport Department was set up for the purpose of providing lorries and vans to transport members of the Women's Land Army and others to and from farms on which they worked. Another of their responsibilities was to teach the young Land Army Girls to drive.

Prisoners of war were also involved and were employed on vehicle maintenance working closely with the department's own mechanics. Eventually the DWAC moved to Heathfield, near Newton Abbot and staff travelled daily until it was disbanded. Tom Herod, the manager, is the imposing figure in the front row.

Among those that can be identified are: Monica Gooch, Winnie Brooks, Doris Metters, Beryl Sarah, Barbara Richards, Doris and Mrs Weeks, Isobel Carew, Barbara Johnson, Ann Houghton, Edie Landick, Mrs Barton, Mrs Yates, Ernie Morrish, Fred Gale, Walter Timms, Tom Cox, Bill Berry, Bert Allen, Wilf Mills, Wally Knight, George Hooper, Sid Bowden, Colin Bowden, Bert Stead, Fred Pillivant. The named ones all lived in Okehampton and surrounding villages, mainly Sticklepath and South Zeal.

THE ROYAL ARTILLERY AT OKEHAMPTON

THE RIGHT OF THE LINE
AND
THE PRIDE OF THE BRITISH ARMY

UBIQUE

1,009

R.H.A

R.F.A

R.G.A

Displayed upon this card you'll see
The Arms of the Royal Artillery;
And in behind you're sure to find
Some splendid views to you consigned.

In the early part of this century there were various "mailing novelty" postcards. This one illustrates the importance of the military on Dartmoor at the Okehampton Battle Camp and featured the R.H.A. (Royal Horse Artillery), R.F.A. (Royal Field Artillery) and R.G.A. (Royal Garrison Artillery). The flap contained no less than 12 popular views of the Okehampton countryside and were much in demand, by locals and holidaymakers alike. At the time this was published this card could be posted for a halfpenny, provided the address of the sender only was written. Any other script then the cost of postage was increased one penny by the GPO. Okehampton really was a "Garrison Town" in those days.

The "Big" guns in use on Dartmoor at the turn of the century and no doubt under training for the Boer War. It was on 9th September 1901 that the greatly respected soldier Field Marshal Earl Roberts V.C. Commander-in-Chief of the British Army arrived at Okehampton for the Artillery camp. The aura surrounding this popular figure could certainly only have been exceeded by the King himself. Earl Roberts was met at the station by the Mayor, members of the entire Corporation, Civic Dignitaries and a veritable crowd of people.

The Mayor (Alderman H. Geen) in a warm welcome said: May it please your lordship in the first place I must thank you on behalf of those present, who are past Mayors, aldermen, and councillors of our ancient borough, for your willingness to grant us this interview. Knowing as we do that the military affairs of this great empire are under your personal control, we cannot fail to be impressed with your great kindness in giving us this opportunity of welcoming you to our fair county of Devon and to our ancient borough of Okehampton. (Applause.) I was present at the Crystal Palace on 23rd May when Lady Roberts unveiled your statue, and feel sure you must have been greatly struck by the precision with which the several military drills on that occasion were carried out by the thousands of our young soldiers and sailors assembled there. But, however important precision of military evolutions in a body may be, in my poor opinion there is an absolute necessity that the British soldier should be trained under conditions approaching as near as possible to actual warfare. I would most respectfully submit to your lordship that such conditions can be more nearly obtained on Dartmoor than elsewhere in the country. (Applause.) And we trust the War-office will utilise more and more the natural advantages of our tors and valleys, not only for artillery, but also for all the other branches of the service. It must follow that soldiers trained under such conditions will be better able to fight the battles of our country in the future than those not having enjoyed some facilities for practice. No doubt, my lord, you have heard of commoners and common rights in connection with the artillery practice on Dartmoor, and that you, together with ourselves, desire that the question of compensation should now be settled, once and for all, so that there should be as it were a fixity of tenure, a certainty of the annual coming of the troops in place of the present uncertainty, which retards the progress of our town. (Applause.) The majority of the commoners would hail with delight the settlement of the question so as to make the camp more permanent; but, of course, there are always a few who object to any settlement except on their own lines, and I would suggest that there is no better way of bringing the whole of the commoners into line than by an Act of Parliament, which should settle not only the amount, but also the fund-rates or otherwise, to which the compensation should go. This, whilst it secures to the Government the right to use the moors for military purposes during certain months, would also secure to the commoners the right which they now enjoy of using the commons at all times when not utilised by the soldiers. At the present time a committee is appointed by the commoners to distribute the compensation moneys received, but before they can obtain the money they are obliged to sign a guarantee indemnifying the War office against all claims for compensation for the commoners. It appears unfair that the committee should be called upon to undertake this liability, and we trust the Government will soon see their way to put the matter on a more satisfactory basis As chief magistrate of the borough I have great pleasure in bearing witness to the general good behaviour of the 8,000 troops who annually pass through the camp hear. (Applause.) It reflects great credit on all concerned and is most important when we remember that this is a health resort as well as a military centre. I cannot conclude without expressing to you our very high appreciation of your distinguished services in South Africa to the empire at large. (Applause.) … Earl Roberts replied: Mr. Mayor and gentlemen, I thank you all most sincerely for your welcome. Okehampton is a place I have very often wished to visit because the troops that have to come here are those belonging to the regiment which I myself was brought up in, and to which I am so proud to belong. (Applause.) I have known the value of Okehampton for many years past, and the various commandants who have been here have told me of its value. Although, of course, I cannot give a direct answer to the matter which you have referred to, I can promise that I will go into the matter carefully, and hope to come to some arrangement by which the Government's interests may be safeguarded as well as the interests of the commoners. I will take the matter up and inquire into it very carefully. I thank you most heartily for your welcome, and am very glad to find myself at Okehampton. (Applause.)

This 1915 photograph may give the impression of a proud family posing with their sons and who were happy to serve king and country during the conflict. Whilst the Lovell family of 62 North Street were certainly proud and loyal, the soldiers were of the North Staffordshire Regiment who had been posted to Okehampton for training on Dartmoor. However there was insufficient accommodation at the battle camp and hundreds of soldiers were billeted in houses throughout the Borough. The patriotic Okehampton families in true Devon spirit wasted no time in making their homes available to these young men. The Horne family at Fairfield House at the bottom of Station Road accommodated no less than 22 soldiers. (Excluding soldiers) Back: William Pike, Mrs Northcott, Miss Day. Front: Mrs Speare, William Lovell, Gertie Lovell, Mrs T. Lovell, Jack Lovell. Unfortunately there was to be no happy ending for the North Staffs as not many of the lads who trained at Okehampton survived the war.

This unique photograph was recovered from a German Bomber, during the 1939-45 war. It clearly shows the Okehampton aerodrome at Folly Gate which was considered an important target.

It appears that if German aircraft were returning following a bombing raid on the larger cities such as Bristol, Plymouth or Exeter and had unused bombs, the pilots were instructed to maximise damage over other areas and Okehampton was certainly one.

When the bombs fell on the evening of Tuesday 1st October 1940, there was no doubt that Okehampton Aerodrome at Folly Gate was the Target area. Despite the damage the Okehampton businessmen were soon displaying their "Business as Usual" signs the following day.

The Aerodrome of course paid host to the then Prince of Wales in the 1920s and in the 1930s featured Sir Alan Cobham's Flying Circus.

The outbreak of War gave the Aerodrome increasing importance. However it seemed like the start of a Ealing Comedy Film when Corporal Martin Staddon and six airmen were posted from RAF Mount Batten to the Folly Gate Aerodrome in January 1940.

They found the Station "Locked Up" and empty, but we are told they enjoyed their stay at the London Hotel where they were billeted! Their job was to establish a Bombing Range on Dartmoor for training purposes.

However the Moor was at its most inhospitable with heavy drifts of snow and great patches of ice. When bombing practice did finally begin the first plane to fly in scored a direct hit with a 250 lbs bomb on the actual target causing it to disappear into the frozen bog on which it had inadvertently been established. This further delayed practice and in combination with the adverse weather conditions only four attempts at target practice were made in three months!

An Okehampton Event, long since abandoned was the motor cycle rally to Land's End and back. This was very well supported, and took place annually on Good Friday, starting in Fore Street at 6:30 a.m. This 1920 picture shows the gathering just before the start, as can be seen by the then Post Office clock. It is rather interesting to note that motorcyclists in those days were members of the business community and more soberly attired than those of today. The Family and Commercial Hotel was a popular hotel for many years before becoming the branch offices of SWEB in 1959. "Marks" the well known bakers were in the shop on the right hand side. The motor cyclists used to take over 12 hours for the return journey, so the first home would be met by a large welcoming crowd at around 7 p.m. The motor cyclists include E. Stinchcombe, Bill Hain, Sid Hain, Harry Newman, Fred Tenby and Mr and Mrs Weaver. Scattered within the crowd are such personalities as: Ginger Hawkins, Orville Maddaford, George Gunn, Jim Crocker, Harold Brooking, Bob Furse, Sid Cann, Arthur Glass, George Heale, Jim Spencer, Harold Day, Fred Metters, Ted Webb, Wallace Day, George Angel, Harry Beer, Claude Cornish, Arthur Bray, Mr and Mrs Backway, Mr and Mrs Miller, Miss Williams and Miss Weaver. No doubt readers will be able to add to this list.

The 1st Okehampton Company of The Girls Life Brigade was initially formed in 1912 and, although disbanded in 1935, was reformed in 1950. This was under the leadership of Miss Joan Pauley who has, through her hard work, contributed much to the life of the town. This 1950s picture shows the large membership at the time. Sadly the company disbanded again in 1972.

Back row, left to right: Trixie Spencer, June Harris, Kath Medland, Jean Crocker, Jean Marles, Diana Lock, Valerie Rees, Josie Marles, Angela Bowerman, Patricia Crocker, Eileen Kelly, Patricia Dawkins, Marcia Day. Middle row: Gillian Hosegood, Sheila Kelly, Hilary Bird, Anita Luxton, Mavis Hosegood, Thelma Aggett, Margaret Barkwill, Miss J. Pauley (captain), Jennifer Hosegood, Janet Brewer, Ann Shaw, Cecily Medland, Bronwyn Lobb, Diana Worden. Front row: Marie Crocker, Rosemary Dawkins, Susan Bulley, Hazel Buxton, Bronwyn Simmons, Pauline Jewell, Pat Goodenough, Beryl Evely, Diane Jenn, Eileen Angel, Judith Powell, Jill Hodge.

The Women's Land Army was reformed in 1939 and it recruited thousands of women to do essential work in farming and forestry. This Okehampton 1948 carnival prizewinning tableau contains two young girls who had come to Okehampton and were to make their homes here. On the far right is Joyce Spiller, who had served for four years in the Wrens prior to joining the Land Army after the war. She met and married Fred Barlow and has been involved much in the life of the church, and also supporting her husband's sterling efforts with the Dartmoor Rescue group. Fred was later to be awarded the BEM. Sylvia Rider (fifth from left) eventually married local personality Harold Westlake, and she could not have anticipated at that time how much she would become involved in civic affairs. First she was elected as a town councillor in 1983, then Sylvia, with Harold as Consort, served as mayor for two years during 1989-91 and again was selected in 1992, 1993 and 1994.

Jeff Cunliffe had arrived with Pembrokeshire Yeomanry in 1942 to be early occupants of the showfield camp. After war service in North Africa he married Peggy, an Okehampton girl, and subsequently returned to the town he loved. Little could Jeff have imagined in those early days, the part he would play in the social and Civic life of the town, becoming mayor in 1976/77. For his initiative and efficiency during the drought, he received recognition from Dennis Howell, the appointed Water Minister. In a career of many accolades, perhaps the highlight was an invitation to visit the Cardinal Archbishop's Palace at Westminster, where amongst others he met Cardinal Hume. This was an honour extended to people who had distinguished themselves in public life. This impressive range of trophies illustrated the outstanding success of the Okehampton motor cycle team of the 296 Field Regt. (R.D.Y) T.A. In 1958

this was celebrated by "dining in" of the regiment at the Drill Hall. (L-R) Bill Penberthy, Bill Lockyer, Col. David Hurn, Major A. S. Harman, Jeff Cunliffe and Brig Ackland. In 19 years of competition this team won countless events culminating in the British Army championships, a feat never accomplished until then by a T.A. Team, although their opponents always felt the team were lucky to have Dartmoor as a "back garden" in which to practice! Summing up, Jeff is a caring and conscientious man who, with the unstinting support of Peggy, has served the community well.

This was a day trip with a difference, for this band of intrepid walkers pictured at Cranmere Pool in 1937. The group had left Okehampton early on a winter's morning with their first stop at Cranmere Pool, where they posed for this photograph. They then proceeded across the moor to Princetown for lunch before making their way to Tavistock and finally returning to Okehampton very late in the evening. An enjoyable if tiring day, although "legend" has it that there was at least one member of the group who suggested that they waited for the last train from Tavistock. There was, of course, one other member – the photographer Harry Newman. Little could he have thought his photograph would be recorded for posterity 70 years on! Back Row (L-R) Bert Marles, Jim Spencer, Sid Casey, Jack Maddaford, Orville Maddaford. Middle Row: Dick Eveleigh, W. F. Day, Bill Lee. Front Row: Harold Day, John Cawse, Jim McIntyre, Les Walters, Arthur Leverton.

One of the out-standing sportsmen produced by Okehampton was W. F. (Bill) Day, a student of Okehampton Grammar School where he was a regular member of the School Soccer Team. It was almost by chance that he discovered his athletic prowess at the Boys' Brigade Sports Championship by beating his close friend Oswald Parker.

W. F. went on to represent Devon in the sprint events on many occasions during the 1920s

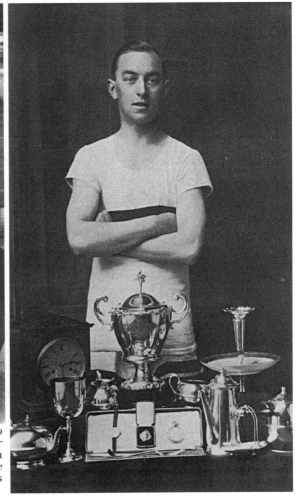

in the South West County Championships with considerable success. He went on to play rugby for Okehampton and later Torquay, whilst his close rivals Oswald Parker and Orville Maddaford represented Okehampton before progressing to Plymouth Albion. He is pictured (right) with some of his major Athletic Trophies whilst above he is in more frivolous mood in Fore Street in the annual Hospital Fête Day, which needless to say he won! The sparkling passenger throughout the race is Gwen Middleton.

It is 10:15 a.m. on 2nd June 1953 as the Borough Council, Civic Dignitaries, the Choir and a packed Fore Street, prepare for the march past on the Coronation Day of Queen Elizabeth II. Amongst those that can be identified on the platform are: The Mayor and Mayoress, Dr C. G. and Mrs Jones, Walter Passmore Snr, Bill Cornish, Les Martin, Rev. Compton, Bill Brock, George Gratton, Clifford Hancock, Bill Backway, J. J. Newcombe and 'Bonzo Studden.' The choir included Kirby Tippett and Harry Sarah who were members for many years. The Council prepared a large official programme for the Coronation, which commenced with Church services on 31st May and 1st June with a full day of events on Coronation Day itself. Various events were held on the 3rd, 4th and 5th and culminated with a musical display with the beating of "The Retreat" on Saturday, 6th June.

This photograph of the 1955 Okehampton Borough Council has been specially selected as it represented a very strong and able municipal body. Packed with experienced business and professional members, it included no less than 10 people who had been, or who would be, Mayor of Okehampton. The Borough Surveyor R. Alan Brunskill, Town Clerk J. J. Newcombe (over 50 years) and W. J. Q. Yeo were an example of the long serving officers, which Okehampton has engendered over so many generations. Back row: (L–R) "Jimmy" Johns, Alan Brunshill (Borough Surveyor), Bill Yeo, "Ginger" Hawkins, Dr C. G. Jones, Dr E. D. Allen-Price, J. J. Newcombe (Town Clerk), Rev. Compton (The Mayor), Rev. Walker, Walter Henry Passmore, Bill Brock, Bill Cornish, Jim Fogaty, Bert Conway. Sitting: Margaret Nash, Reg Horne, Oswald Parker, Ron Bray, Bill Letchford, Harry Cleverdon, Bert Richmond, Walter John Passmore, Clem White, Iris Kennard.

The Okehampton Borough Band reformed after the war with the triumphant serviceman returning to less dangerous activities under the direction of a conductor rather than the discipline of a Sergeant Major! This Springtime photograph shows them posing in their new uniforms prior to a major competition. They had raised the money for these uniforms by a variety of events. However, in those days it was not just the money, but the collection of "clothing coupons" that was needed to fulfil this project. Due to the unstinting support of the townsfolk, both targets were duly accomplished. It will be noticed that there is a solitary lady in the band, namely the jolly Audrey Friend, who was the first female admitted to this previously male-dominated group of musicians. That she did so was due entirely to her persistence, and even then it required an extraordinary general meeting of the band to gain approval! Well done Audrey!

(L–R) Reg Maddaford, Dick Mills, Digger Stoneman, George Bird, George Partington, Bill Crocker, Peter Evans, Bill Bird, Wyndham Tremlett, Les Walters, Jack Smale, Ben Luxton, Audrey Friend, Gerald Rendle, Mr Ogden (Conductor), Bill Clark, Jim Crocker, Sid Webber, Jack Kelly, Eric Jordan, Tommy Bevan, Bill Doble, Jim Bulley, Rex Voaden and Harold Bevan.

The Okehampton Amateur Operatic and Dramatic Society certainly existed in various guises since the last century although there is no suggestion that the "lovely ladies" in the above 1920s photograph were involved in that time!

In November 1897 the society performed a thrilling drama, "Foiled by a Fool," to a packed house with the proceeds being devoted to the new Rifle Range for the Volunteers.

Throughout its long life the society always supported charities; as long ago as the Boer War they provided entertainment in support of funds for families of our soldiers and sailors.

Chorus: (L-R) Back Row: Mary Brunskill, Gwen Loram, Mabel Wotton, (unknown).
Middle: Mrs Jack Day, Rene Quance, Ethel Quance, France Yeo.
Front: Gertie Horne, Kathleen Down.

History has recorded the flood disaster that struck the picturesque Devon village of Lynmouth on the night of 15/16th August 1952, with its sad loss of life and widespread damage. Dartmoor and Okehampton too, experienced torrential rain and both East and West Ockments rose with frightening rapidity. Many areas around the rivers were flooded to high levels with the roads awash. The Okehampton Fire Brigade, as always, were quickly into action and equal to the task as the above photograph at the Gas works illustrates. Coincidentally, the young lad on the left is young Tony Lowe who was destined for a career with British Gas!

The 1920/1921 Boys' Brigade Reserve (Juniors) pose for the camera in Simmons Park under their Captain, Mr Edward Stinchcombe.
Rear: Sid Vernon. Back Row: John Hawkins, Albert Pedrick, Bill Cornish, Frank Searle, Bert Hawkins, Claude Cockwill.
2nd Row: Bob Furse, Henry Hooper, Les Taylor, Arthur Welham, Jim Cockwill, Nelson Netherway, Les Hooper, Tom Sims.
Front Row: Ern Day, Ern Dymond, Eddie Lee (on drum), Bill Bubear, Bert Cockwill, E. Day, Joe Newcombe, Bill Ruby.
On the extreme left is Stan Drew, a popular Okehampton businessman for many years.

T. Day & Sons Ltd, Okehampton with their workshops and offices situated in New Road had established a reputation as leading motor engineers. However, with their highly skilled and experienced staff they were very versatile and innovative in their work. One challenge of course was the annual Okehampton Carnival and this 1922 entry was typical of their efforts. Perhaps encouraged by the fact that two of their staff were ex-matelots, this gunboat tableaux was awarded first prize in its category, at a time when the British Fleet ruled the waves.

Jack Day (sitting by gun), Bill Walters (Ex-sailor), Frank Horn (Foreman), Fred Day (Director of Days and naturally Captain), Tom Cox (Ex-Sailor), Horace Weaver (Rear Gunner). One wonders whether this tableaux with its obvious motive power would be allowed on the road today without tax and insurance.

Whilst the staff at T. Day & Sons Ltd created a float for the carnival by voluntary efforts in their own time, they received every encouragement from the Directors who made every facility and a bay available. In addition the directors with true public spiritedness and a civic duty provided a coach and driver for the carnival Queen at the firm's expense. Certainly together with coaches for the Mayor and Councillors this 1922 coach, which had replaced the horse-drawn carriage, made a marvellous sight in full colour. A replica crown adorned the roof of the coach with the decorative colours varying from white to pale pink to crimson. These colours were repeated on the wheels, and the wheel arches and the running boards were covered in green leaves. A Ford Model "T" car was selected, the problem set to the engineers was to provide 20 revolving lights on each wheel. This was finally achieved with a great deal of ingenuity and experimentation. A similar coach today would be much admired. The efforts of "Days" were repeated for many years and the staff looked forward to their "Annual Challenge."

The season is 1922/23 and the successful Okehampton Boys' School football team line up for the camera with their teachers. The team had just won the trophy for the third time. Back row (L – R): Mr Betts (Headmaster), A. Marles, C. Cockwill, C. Letchford, Mr Vanstone (Teacher). Middle row: S. Luxton, R. Burt, F. Hill, C. Johns, W. Medland, F. Barkwill, Mr Heard (Teacher). Front row: O. Maddaford, J. Howard, L. Yeo, F. Linscott, H. Hawkins.

A study of Miss Gale's Class of 1929 taken outside the Okehampton Primary School in North Street. Back Row (L-R): Ernie Hunt, Albert Pedrick, Thora Beer, Leonard Matters, Reggie Webber, Victor Sparkes, Jim Slee. Middle Row: Ernest Bassett, Rachael Cornish, Edna Barkwell, Evelyn Littlejohns, Renee Beer, Edie Squires. Front Row: Dorothy Squires, Evelyn Power, Bernie Guscott, Barbara Letchford, Norah Webber, Phyllis Knott. Teacher centre: Miss V. Gale. This Victorian school (now closed) was built at a cost of £1,670 for 400 pupils, and provided sound education for successive generations of Okehampton children.

John Hutchings & Son traded as Machine Bakers, Pastry Cooks and Confectioners at their premises at 9 West Street. One man who contributed much to their success was Harry Down who worked for "Hutchings" for sixty years as a baker's roundsman.
This 1910 picture shows Harry about to set off on his rounds, which covered the Okehampton Borough and the rural areas. He took great pride in his work and his loyalty was such that he seldom missed a day through ill health. Although on one occasion, suffering from rheumatic fever, he cocooned himself in blankets and insisted on accompanying the relief roundsman for several days so he could become familiar with the routes and customers. The telephone service was connected to Okehampton at this time and "Hutchings" became Okehampton No 13, a number retained for many years.

This article first appeared in the Okehampton Times in October 1982.

JAMES PIPER, A MAN OF SIZE AND NOTE

One of the best known of Okehampton citizens at the turn of the century was James Piper: He was not the Mayor of Okehampton, not the Town Clerk, not even a Councillor. In fact, Okehampton at that time boasted a Town Porter and James Piper more than filled the post. He was instantly recognized because of his tremendous size, and was known not only by residents of Okehampton but also by the many visitors to the Moorland town. He became even better known when he was featured on post cards, like the one reproduced on this page. James, as he preferred to be called, rather than Jimmy, was born in Monkokehampton, but moved to Okehampton when very young and quickly acquired the status of a local celebrity because of his ample proportions and a prodigious appetite. He occupied various positions in the town, sustaining and expanding both his gastronomic reputation and his massive size. He was given the position of Town Porter and was also attached to the White Hart Hotel when the proprietor was Mr. Heywood. He would often go with the regular hotel coach to the busy Okehampton Station and help in all ways with passengers and luggage, as well as freight. Although he had a slow and somewhat lazy gait, James did not altogether shirk work, and when the dire needs of his stomach demanded it, he was not above cracking a few stones to earn an honest copper. However, he was not to enjoy a long life. He died when only 39 years old in January 1907. Immediately his friends opened a subscription list which was well received and supported and very soon Mr J. J. Marles, sculptor, of New Road, Okehampton, was commissioned to provide a suitable monument. The stone was soon erected and the inscription was as follows: James Piper Town Porter who died 21st January 1907 aged 39 years. In the midst of life we are in death. Erected in token of regard by some of his friends. James was a simple good hearted chap, with many friends and no enemies.

The Okehampton Congregational chapel in North Street provided much spiritual help and enjoyment over so many generations. It is not generally known that the "membership" was such that a football team was regularly fielded. This one, dated around 1910, included some of the young men of the day, many of whom were soon to play an important part in the business life of the borough.
Back row: Frank Cornish, Harold Wright, George Drew, Claude Cornish, Arthur Glass, Bill Weeks, Mr Day, the Rev. Nicholas Oliver.
Centre row: Leo Sprague, H. Harris.
Front row: John Howard, 'Cockbird' Williams, Charlie Ward, Reg Lugg, Bert Allin.

The Okehampton Cricket Club in 1930 featured considerable talent. The dashing-looking man wearing the cravat seated on the left was the young Derek Brown. He was to succeed his father H. C. Brown as president (two places to the right) in 1938 and held that office for 45 years, surely a record?

Others that can be easily identified are Dr Sharp, Jack Williams, Dick Mills, Gerald Furse, Eddie and Courtenay Ash, Albert Palmer and Bill Lee. The young man in the suit on the left is Jack Acton who acted as groundsman, and remembered working five evenings a week on pitch preparation for a total of ten shillings (50p).

Seated on the right of the board advertising a dance is a man known as "Drover Bill" of no fixed address but professing to be an advertising executive as he toured the town with his advertising boards.

This formal group shows the Okehampton Bowling Club in 1927. We have been able to identify most of the people in the photograph, but the ratio between men and women is rather noticeable. Perhaps the gentler sex in those days were not encouraged to play, but welcomed for the preparation of tea?

Back row (L–R): Harris, Bellamy, (?), G. Eveleigh, T. Jordan, H. E. White, R. Lintern, H. Yeo, (?), J. Ruby, J. Hutchings, Oliver, W. Smale.

Third row: Harding, (?), Lashmere, J. Billett, W. Martin, A. E. Smale, Bert Bulley, W. H. Backway, Dr Burd, E. Stinchcombe, R. Finch, A. E. Bailey, Penwells, A. Powlesland, P. Edgcumbe, W. Avery.

Second row: (?), (?), Bill Yeo, A. W. Coles, J. J. Newcombe, Weaver, Miss Rowe, (?).

Front row: S. Piper, W. J. Q. Yeo, T. Holmes, T. Day, A. E. Worden, C. O'Brien, J. Vanstone, W. J. Hutchings Snr, A. Doble, F. Kelly.

This photograph of the 1937 Okehampton Social Club is reminiscent of a prewar Hollywood film set. They certainly lead a busy sporting and social life. Tennis was the most popular sport with a court hired from "Strouds" greengrocers in Fore Street at the end of their gardens leading towards the present Market car park. In the winter months the Market Hall was used for badminton and in addition a room in East Street was hired for table tennis, darts, cards, cribbage, bridge and no doubt more than the occasional cup of tea and coffee.

Back Row: Douglas Weaver, Richard (Dick) Eveleigh, Bertie Smale, Walter Boucher, Charlie O'Brien, Berkly Williams, Gertie Williams, Joan Eveleigh, and two unknown.

Second row: Gertie Horne, Phil Pellow, Mrs Williams, Ann Gaw.

Front: Mrs Smale, Lily Hain, Phil McIntyre, Milly Pike, Chrissie Stoneman. It is sad that the outbreak of war brought to a halt the activities of this happy group.

Careful study of this group beating the bounds of Belstone taken near Culliver Steps on 14th June 1923 shows that some taking part were fully intent on enjoying themselves. As an example, the flagon of cider in the right hand of the character just off centre and "the piratical" gentleman on the far right with the shot gun in the "slope arms" position.
*Judging by the costumes it was certainly not **flaming June**!*

There are few photographs of the Rattlebrook Peat Works or the Rattlebrook Railway Line, but this one of the loading siding reveals it was a major employer of local labour. There were exceptionally large peat beds at Rattlebrook and there were great hopes that these could be exploited by the West of England Compressed Peat Company, as tar oil, acetic acid, naptha and even petrol, as well as other products that could be manufactured from peat. The Rattlebrook Track, unusually for a Moorland line, was standard gauge and although the works was only 2½ miles from Bridestowe Station, it was necessary for a railway line of 5 miles to overcome the gradient. It was at the end of the 1914–18 war that T. Day & Sons Ltd, the well known Okehampton Engineers, designed and purpose-built a petrol engine to pull the trucks and replace the horses, which had struggled for years. Various attempts have been made over the years to economically make use of the peat beds but alas with little success. One story we like is that of a German Scientist, told to us by an expert Moorman. It appears many years ago this scientist would work long hours by flickering candle light, perfecting his formula for producing alcohol, but much to the disappointment of "The Locals" he died without revealing his secret!

Albany Savile built the Oaklands Manor, and naturally the construction of a building of such magnificence in the last century caused a great deal of interest. This excerpt appeared in the Trewman's Exeter Flying Post on 27th December 1821. Albany Savile and his family were great benefactors to the town, and for many those in need benefited from the "Annual Savile Gift."

On Monday last, at Oaklands, in the parish of Okehampton, in this county, Albany Savile, Esq. gave a dinner to the whole of the mechanics and labourers, upwards of one hundred, who have been employed in building the stupendous mansion which he now occupies at that place; a temporary room was fitted out for the occasion, decorated with evergreens, and at two o'clock the dinner, which consisted of Old English fare, was lain out; the principal dish, a

We will all drink to that!

Baron of Beef, was carried from the house to the room by four servants, in livery and white aprons, preceded by an excellent band, and followed by the whole of the company in files. The music continued to play the whole time, and a quantity of seats were erected, in an elevated situation, on which the principal part of the Ladies and Gentlemen of the town sat to witness the scene. After the cloth was removed a plentiful supply of strong beer and spirits was given to

them; and in the evening they were joined by their wives and sweethearts, when, with the assistance of the band and the Jolly God Bacchus, they danced on the "light fantastic toe" until eleven o'clock, at which time (it being Xmas Eve) they all quietly dispersed, chanting songs of blessing and praise to their charitable benefactor, who by means of his bounty, and good arrangement, so amply administered to the wants and cheered the hearts of a portion of his fellow creatures.